```
940.54  Skipper, G. C.
SKI
        Submarines in the
        Pacific
```

DATE			
JAN 19 '82	De 11 1986		
FEB 2 '82	Nc 20 1987		
FEB 15 '82	Oc 4 1988		
APR 28 '82			
FEB 1 '83			
MAR 16 '83			
APR 27 '83			
MAY 19 '83			
JAN 19 '84			
MAR 14 '84			
MAR 21 '84			
Nc 14 1985			

McDONOUGH MIDDLE SCHOOL LIBRARY

© THE BAKER & TAYLOR CO.

McDonough Middle School Library

SOME MAJOR EVENTS IN WORLD WAR II

THE EUROPEAN THEATER

1939 SEPTEMBER—Germany invades Poland; Great Britain, France, Australia, & New Zealand declare war on Germany; Battle of the Atlantic begins. NOVEMBER—Russia invades Finland.

1940 APRIL—Germany invades Denmark & Norway. MAY—Germany invades Belgium, Luxembourg, & The Netherlands; British forces retreat to Dunkirk and escape to England. JUNE—Italy declares war on Britain & France; France surrenders to Germany. JULY—Battle of Britain begins. SEPTEMBER—Italy invades Egypt; Germany, Italy, & Japan form the Axis countries. OCTOBER—Italy invades Greece. NOVEMBER—Battle of Britain over. DECEMBER—Britain attacks Italy in North Africa.

1941 JANUARY—Allies take Tobruk. FEBRUARY—Rommel arrives at Tripoli. APRIL—Germany invades Greece & Yugoslavia. JUNE—Allies are in Syria; Germany invades Russia. JULY—Russia joins Allies. AUGUST—Germans capture Kiev. OCTOBER—Germany reaches Moscow. DECEMBER—Germans retreat from Moscow; Japan attacks Pearl Harbor; United States enters war against Axis nations.

1942 MAY—first British bomber attack on Cologne. JUNE—Germans take Tobruk. SEPTEMBER—Battle of Stalingrad begins. OCTOBER—Battle of El Alamein begins. NOVEMBER—Allies recapture Tobruk; Russians counterattack at Stalingrad.

1943 JANUARY—Allies take Tripoli. FEBRUARY—German troops at Stalingrad surrender. APRIL—revolt of Warsaw Ghetto Jews begins. MAY—German and Italian resistance in North Africa is over; their troops surrender in Tunisia; Warsaw Ghetto revolt is put down by Germany. JULY—allies invade Sicily; Mussolini put in prison. SEPTEMBER—Allies land in Italy; Italians surrender; Germans occupy Rome; Mussolini rescued by Germany. OCTOBER—Allies capture Naples; Italy declares war on Germany. NOVEMBER—Russians recapture Kiev.

1944 JANUARY—Allies land at Anzio. JUNE—Rome falls to Allies; Allies land in Normandy (D-Day). JULY—assassination attempt on Hitler fails. AUGUST—Allies land in southern France. SEPTEMBER—Brussels freed. OCTOBER—Athens liberated. DECEMBER—Battle of the Bulge.

1945 JANUARY—Russians free Warsaw. FEBRUARY—Dresden bombed. APRIL—Americans take Belsen and Buchenwald concentration camps; Russians free Vienna; Russians take over Berlin; Mussolini killed; Hitler commits suicide. MAY—Germany surrenders; Goering captured.

THE PACIFIC THEATER

1940 SEPTEMBER—Japan joins Axis nations Germany & Italy.

1941 APRIL—Russia & Japan sign neutrality pact. DECEMBER—Japanese launch attacks against Pearl Harbor, Hong Kong, the Philippines, & Malaya; United States and Allied nations declare war on Japan; China declares war on Japan, Germany, & Italy; Japan takes over Guam, Wake Island, & Hong Kong; Japan attacks Burma.

1942 JANUARY—Japan takes over Manila; Japan invades Dutch East Indies. FEBRUARY—Japan takes over Singapore; Battle of the Java Sea. APRIL—Japanese overrun Bataan. MAY—Japan takes Mandalay; Allied forces in Philippines surrender to Japan; Japan takes Corregidor; Battle of the Coral Sea. JUNE—Battle of Midway; Japan occupies Aleutian Islands. AUGUST—United States invades Guadalcanal in the Solomon Islands.

1943 FEBRUARY—Guadalcanal taken by U.S. Marines. MARCH—Japanese begin to retreat in China. APRIL—Yamamoto shot down by U.S. Air Force. MAY—U.S. troops take Aleutian Islands back from Japan. JUNE—Allied troops land in New Guinea. NOVEMBER—U.S. Marines invade Bougainville & Tarawa.

1944 FEBRUARY—Truk liberated. JUNE—Saipan attacked by United States. JULY—battle for Guam begins. OCTOBER—U.S. troops invade Philippines; Battle of Leyte Gulf won by Allies.

1945 JANUARY—Luzon taken; Burma Road won back. MARCH—Iwo Jima freed. APRIL—Okinawa attacked by U.S. troops; President Franklin Roosevelt dies; Harry S. Truman becomes president. JUNE—United States takes Okinawa. AUGUST—atomic bomb dropped on Hiroshima; Russia declares war on Japan; atomic bomb dropped on Nagasaki. SEPTEMBER—Japan surrenders.

McDonough Middle School Library

WORLD AT WAR

Submarines in the Pacific

WORLD AT WAR

Submarines in the Pacific

By G.C. Skipper

 CHILDRENS PRESS, CHICAGO

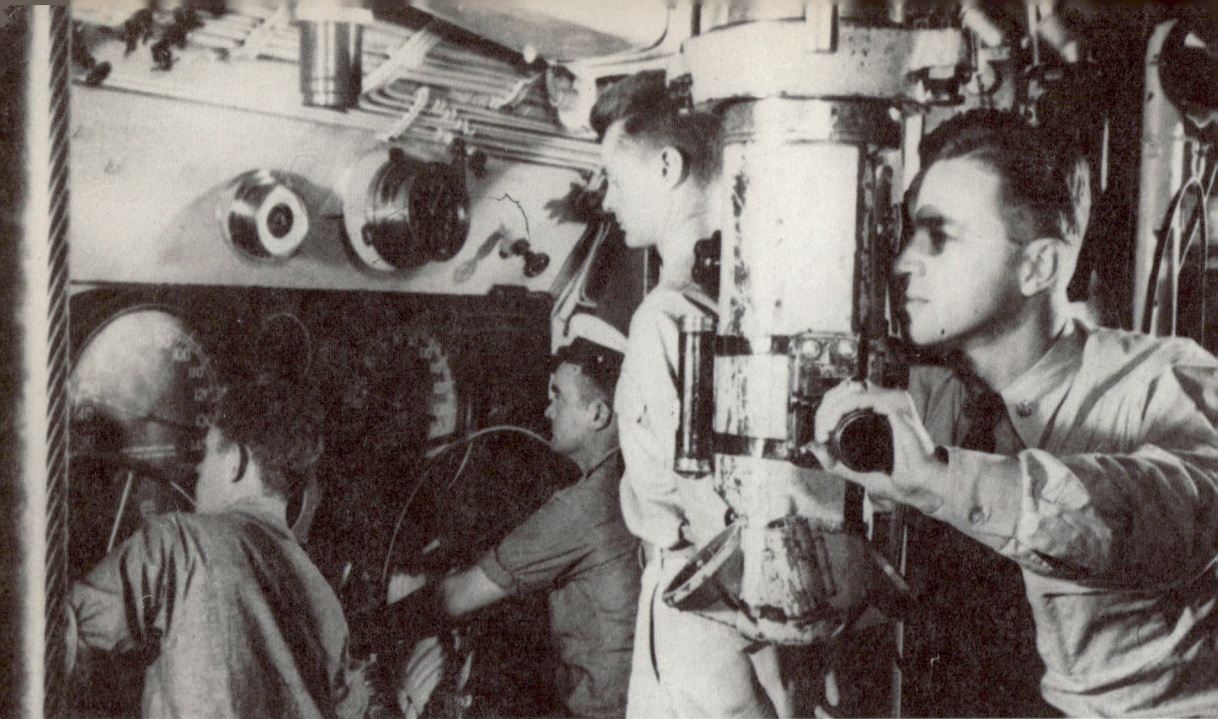

A submarine commander scans the Pacific Ocean horizon through a periscope. When Commander J.R. "Dinty" Moore looked through his periscope on the *S-44* he saw four Japanese cruisers returning from the Battle of Savo Island in the Solomons.

FRONTISPIECE:
Crew members of the submarine *Wahoo* help out survivors of a becalmed fishing vessel with food and water. The *Wahoo* had been out on a war patrol and had sunk a Japanese destroyer and a convoy of four ships.

Library of Congress Cataloging in Publication Data

Skipper, G.C.
  Submarines in the Pacific.

  (His World at war)
  SUMMARY: Describes the role of American submarines during World War II as they patrolled the Pacific Ocean in deadly wolf packs.
  1. World War, 1939-1945—Naval operations—Submarine—Juvenile literature. 2. World War, 1939-1945—Naval operations, American—Juvenile literature. 3. World War, 1939-1945—Pacific Ocean—Juvenile literature. [1. World War, 1939-1945—Naval operations—Submarine. 2. World War, 1939-1945—Naval operations, American. 3. World War, 1939-1945—Pacific Ocean] I. Title. II. Series.
D783.S57   940.54'5973   80-17178
  ISBN 0-516-04786-8

Copyright© by Regensteiner Publishing Enterprises, Inc.
All rights reserved. Published simultaneously in Canada.
Printed in the United States of America.
1 2 3 4 5 6 7 8 9 10 R 87 86 85 84 83 82 81 80

PICTURE CREDITS:
OFFICIAL U.S. NAVY PHOTOGRAPH: Cover, pages 11, 14, 22, 24, 32, 34, 46
UPI: pages 4, 13, 15, 17, 20, 26, 31
NATIONAL ARCHIVES: pages 6, 8, 18, 35, 37, 39, 41, 43, 45
LEN MEENTS (map): page 28

COVER PHOTO:
The carrier U.S.S. *Cavalla*

The periscope suddenly popped out of the water. It resembled a strange snake turning its head first to one side, then the other. The periscope stopped. It focused in on something moving across the wide stretch of the Pacific. The periscope became very still.

Down below, hidden beneath the water, John Raymond Moore, nicknamed "Dinty," turned his eye away from the periscope.

"Take a look at this," Dinty Moore said.

One of the officers on Moore's submarine, the *S-44*, placed his eye to the glass. The officer gave a low whistle. "What have we here?" the officer asked.

"We'll know in a moment," Moore said. "Alert the crew."

The officer moved aside. He shouted orders in the closeness of the submarine. Moore again stared through the periscope. What he saw was unbelievable. Four Japanese cruisers were confidently sailing along on their way home. They were the same ships that had badly damaged the

This photo of a sinking Japanese ship was taken through the periscope of the submarine whose torpedoes had done the damage.

United States Navy a short time before during the Battle of Savo Island in the Solomons.

Moore watched the ships. He waited. The first ship passed. Then the second. Around him Moore could feel the anxiety of his crew. He knew they were wondering why he didn't fire. Still Moore waited. The third Japanese ship came into view, then disappeared.

Suddenly Moore zeroed in on the fourth Japanese ship, the last one in line. "Fire!" he shouted.

The first torpedo shot out of the tube.

"Fire!" Moore commanded.

The second torpedo cut across the water in a silent, swishing sound.

"Fire!" came the order again. And once more, "Fire!"

All four torpedoes raced across the water. The first one hit the Japanese ship. There was a shattering explosion. The submarine was 700 yards away when the torpedo struck.

Every boiler on the ship exploded. The noise was so terrifying that Moore's crew on the *S-44* were panic stricken.

"Dive!" shouted Moore. "Let's get out of here!"

Immediately the Japanese began dropping depth charges. They were trying to hit the American sub. The explosions rocked the submarine. But the depth charges were not nearly so terrifying to the crew of the *S-44* as the horrible hissing noise.

It seemed as if something were dragging across the hull of the submarine. It rocked and tossed. For a moment, the crew members thought their own water and air lines had been ripped away. The men on the *S-44* thought they were about to die. Moore took the *S-44* down and manuevered it, rocking and tossing, away from the horrible hissing sound.

Soon the sub leveled out and all was quiet again down beneath the water. Above them, the

The gun crew of Dinty Moore's submarine, the *S-44*

Japanese cruiser *Kaku* was going down. Its boilers hissed loudly as it plunged toward the bottom of the sea.

The date was August 10, 1942. The *S-44* had just been the first United States submarine to sink a major Japanese combat ship in World War II.

United States submarines were destined to play a crucial role in the war against Japan. During

11

1942, 1943, and 1944 the subs proved to be the decisive factor that crushed Japan's economy. This was done by the sinking of Japanese merchant ships. The merchant ships were responsible for bringing raw material into Japan. These raw materials were necessary to the country. They made it possible for the tiny island to keep up her war production and her fight against the Allies.

United States submarines scurried all across the Pacific. They blasted away enemy military ships. They formed blockades, defended coastlines, and conducted commando raids. They also laid underwater mines and delivered supplies to Allied troops in the heat of battle.

American submarines were also important in rescuing flyers who had to ditch into the Pacific when their planes were shot out of the sky. The subs played just as important a role in rescuing United States sailors stranded at sea.

During 1942, the first year United States submarines entered World War II, a total of 350

American submarines played an important part in rescuing flyers who had been shot down over the Pacific. The submarine *Tang*, under Lieutenant Commander Richard H. O'Kane, rescued twenty-two fliers who were shot down off the Japanese base, Truk. This photo was taken during the two-day rescue operation.

war patrols were sent out. Dinty Moore's *S-44* was only one of these war patrols. It did very well.

But the overall batting average of these early sub patrols was not good. One of the reasons was that the commanders that year were inexperienced and overcautious. That first year only two major Japanese ships were sunk. One was the heavy

13

cruiser *Kaku*, sunk by Dinty Moore. The other was a light cruiser, the *Tenryu*. The *Tenryu* was blasted out of the water by the United States submarine *Albacore*.

The Japanese, on the other hand, sank the carriers *Yorktown*, the *Wasp*, and the *Saratoga*. They badly damaged many other American ships.

The United States aircraft carrier *Yorktown* is shown here after being badly damaged by Japanese torpedoes. The ship later went down.

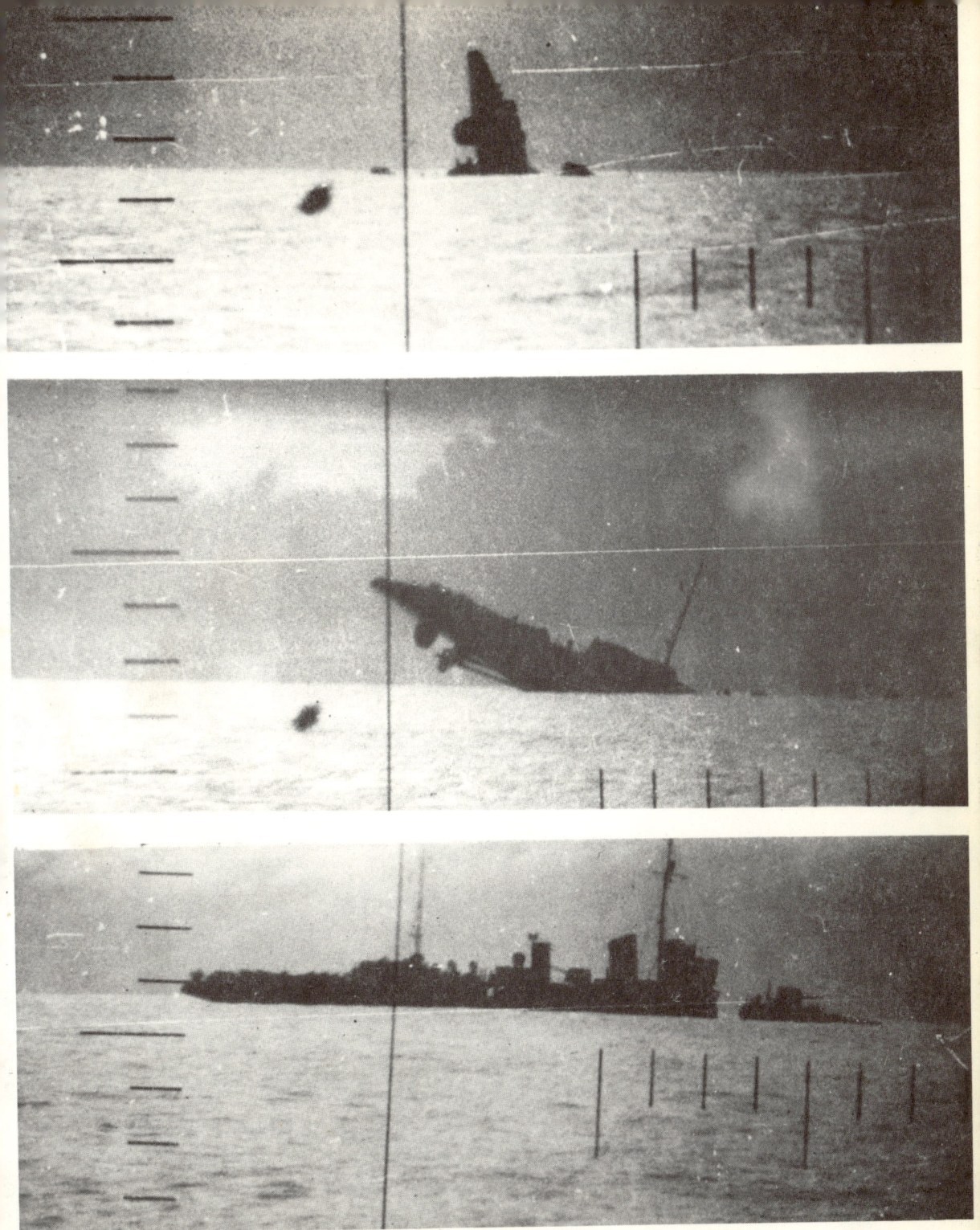

These periscope photos show the sinking of a Japanese destroyer by an American submarine.

But things changed rapidly for the Americans. The second year of the underwater war in the Pacific was to be a much better year. The Americans were using an important fighting strategy—the "wolf pack." These were small bands of submarines that went out to hunt down the enemy.

The wolf-pack strategy had been originated by the Germans. Rear Admiral Karl Doenitz was the German submarine fleet commander. In the Battle of the Atlantic, his U-boats were formed into large attack groups. They were very effective against Allied shipping. The Americans used Doenitz's idea. But the American sub groups were smaller. Usually there were no more than four American submarines in a group.

During 1942 the American wolf packs had merely searched out the enemy. Now there were three new commanders heading up submarine warfare. They were Charles Andrews Lockwood, Jr., Ralph Waldo Christie, and James Fife.

Charles Andrews Lockwood, Jr., commander of the submarine force of the United states Pacific fleet.

Vice Admiral Charles Lockwood with Dick O'Kane, commanding officer of the U.S.S. *Tang*.

These three commanders knew what had to be done if United States submarines were to be effective in the war. The wolf packs had to attack, not just locate, enemy ships. The greatest danger in this war strategy was that United States subs might very well sink friendly ships.

But it was a risk that had to be taken. Lockwood sent 50 percent of his Pearl Harbor submarine fleet into the East China Sea and the Pacific coastal waters off Japan. He also recognized that the Luzon Strait created a bottleneck for Japanese ships. He sent wolf packs into that area as well.

Meanwhile Christie and Fife pinpointed known Japanese shipping lanes. They sent their subs into those regions to stop the supply of raw material.

Again, in 1943, the Americans sent out 350 war patrols, the same number launched in 1942. Thanks to wolf packing, 1943 was a much better year. United States subs sank more than 300 Japanese ships, a 100 percent increase in tonnage sunk over 1942. These sinkings hurt the Japanese badly. Imports to the Land of the Rising Sun dropped sharply.

American submarines waged a mighty war against Japanese shipping. This photo of a Japanese merchant ship was taken through the periscope of the United States submarine that was about to torpedo her.

The Japanese were stung by the severe damage of the United States submarines. They lashed back viciously. The enemy sank twice as many American subs in the Pacific in 1943 as they did in 1942.

As 1943 moved toward its end, the fighting became even more fierce. On November 30 three Japanese aircraft carriers left their fleet base on Truk Island in the Carolines. They were headed for Japan. The carriers were the *Zuiho* and two escort carriers, *Chuyo* and *Unyo*.

The three Japanese ships ran at high speed across the Pacific. They zig-zagged in the submarine-infested waters. They moved swiftly as they headed for the safety of their home port.

On December 2 the zig-zagging enemy ships were spotted by Junior McCain just off Iwo Jima. McCain's submarine was 6,000 yards away. He closed up the gap and dived, readying his crew to attack.

As McCain was preparing to fire the first of his torpedoes, the *Zuiho* suddenly cut sharply. It bore down on McCain's sub.

"They're headed straight at us!" one of McCain's officers yelled.

"Dive!" shouted McCain. "Take her down! Quick!"

The diving officer and two enlisted men prepare to send this submarine into a dive. Diving procedures were the same on Junior McCain's submarine, the *Gunnel*, as it went down to avoid the *Zuiho*.

McCain's sub, the *Gunnel*, headed for the bottom of the ocean. There was no other choice. If the American submarine had not dived the ships would have collided. All the Americans would have been killed.

22

Because of the steep dive to get out of the way, McCain was not able to fire one shot at the Japanese ships. He could only radio the incident to his superiors.

Another submarine commander, Bob Ward, happened to be located a little further north of McCain, right off Japan. Ward and the crew of the *Sailfish* picked up the message about the Japanese ships.

But the *Sailfish* had its own problems at the moment. The submarine was in the middle of a winter typhoon. The sea was extremely rough. It raged and foamed. The sub was whipped around without mercy.

Despite the storm, Ward managed to get *Sailfish* into a position to intercept the Japanese ships.

For one entire day Ward and his crew lay submerged out of sight. They were waiting for the Japanese.

The typhoon and the churning ocean forced the Japanese ships to stop zig-zagging. When they

Bob Ward's submarine, the *Sailfish*, as she looked eight months before her run-in with the Japanese aircraft carriers

reached the waters where the *Sailfish* waited, the enemy ships were moving in a straight line.

Finally, at the end of the day, Ward ordered the submarine to surface. Gradually it made its way to the top of the ocean. When it popped out, Ward found to his dismay that the typhoon was still raging. Huge waves rolled and pitched like things gone mad. The wind howled and screamed and tossed the *Sailfish* around.

"Can't see a thing in this storm!" shouted one of the crew members. "If they're out there we wouldn't know it!"

Suddenly there was a blip on the radar screen. "Look at that!" Ward said, pointing to the screen. The radar screen blipped again. "Something's out there," said Ward, "about 9,000 yards away!"

Immediately Ward gave the command for the *Sailfish* to dive. The submarine disappeared under the water as the typhoon continued to howl and screech.

Then Ward began the waiting game. He held the sub below the surface of the water and

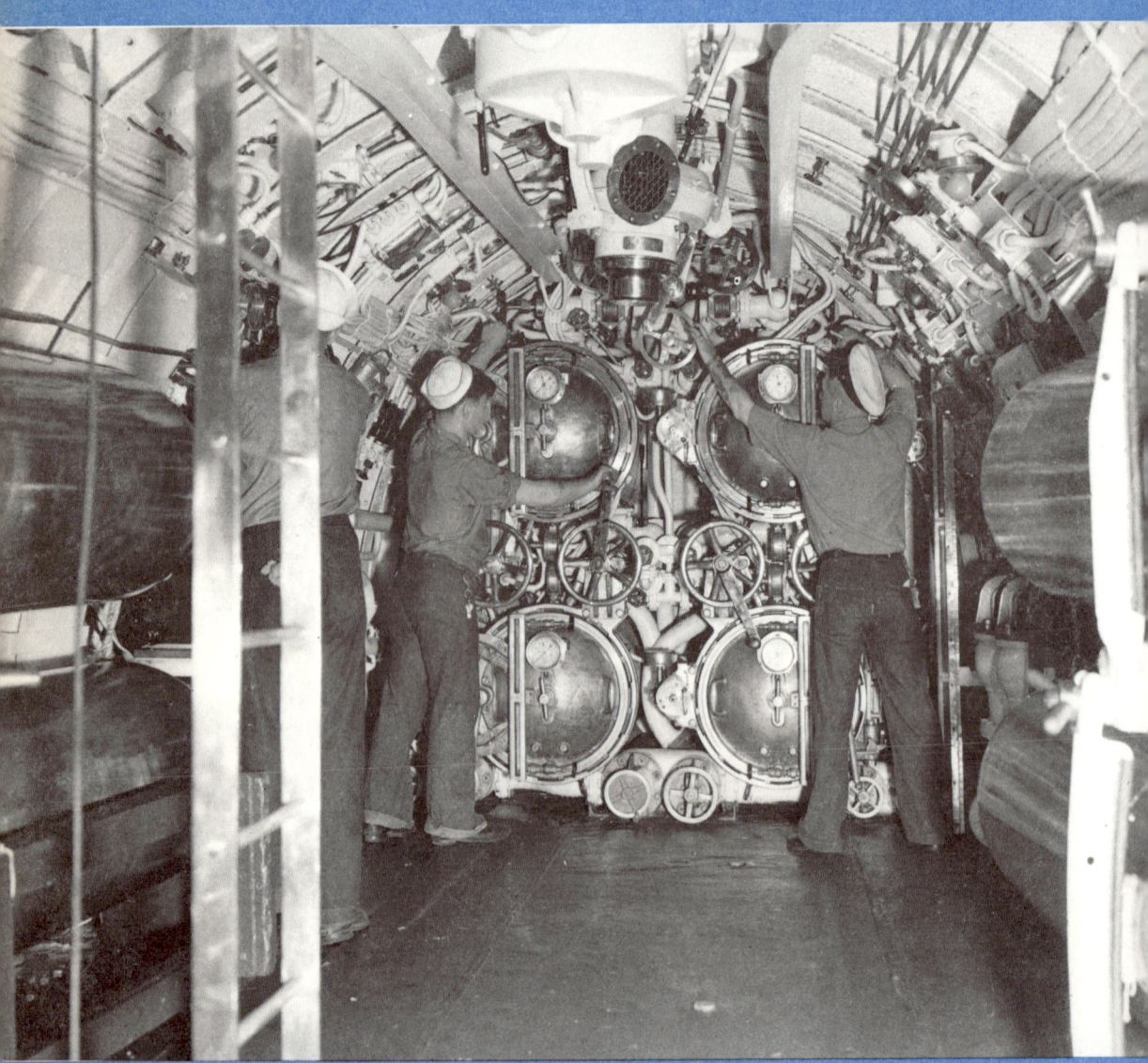

In a typical submarine torpedo room, men are operating the controls of the four torpedo tubes. Other torpedoes are stacked at the sides of the room.

watched the radar screen. When the Japanese ships were only 2,100 yards away, Ward yelled, "Fire!" Four torpedoes cut out of the tubes of the bow. The target was one of the largest ships on the radar screen.

There were two solid hits.

"That's the way to do it!" yelled a crew member of the *Sailfish*.

But before the excitement of the hit could go any further, someone yelled, "What's that?"

Suddenly, out of the darkness, a huge Japanese destroyer came roaring toward the sub. Ward had to act quickly or else be run over.

"Dive deeper!" he commanded. "Take her all the way down!"

The *Sailfish* hightailed it toward the bottom of the ocean. The Japanese destroyer hurled twenty-one depth charges down on her. The explosions ripped through the water. Two of the depth charges fell very, very close to the *Sailfish*. The submarine rocked and shuddered dangerously.

The depth charges were exploding all around the submarine. Ward ordered his men to reload the torpedo tubes. When the tubes were loaded, Ward waited.

After awhile the depth charges stopped. The *Sailfish* bobbed and tossed unhurt beneath the water.

"Take her up," Ward commanded.

It was two o'clock in the morning when the *Sailfish* eased again to the surface. Ward again checked his radar screen to find out what was out there in the darkness. The screen was filled with blips.

One of the blips, however, moved very slowly. "I don't know what we hit, but there it is," he told one of his officers. He pointed to the slow-moving blip. "We hit her good, too," he added.

"What kind of ship is it?" the officer asked.

"Can't tell," said Ward. "Let's track it down and find out."

The *Sailfish* began to track the slow-moving blip on the screen. Ward ordered the *Sailfish* into firing position. He continued stalking the slow-moving target.

He was still tracking it when dawn came. The first light of early morning streaked the sky. The water glinted with light as the sun caught the ripples on the surface.

"Let's hit her again," Ward said, watching the target. He ordered three more torpedoes to be fired.

Barely were the torpedoes out of the tubes when two of them hit the target. There was a great swoosh of fire. It erupted like a fountain of flame from the top of a volcano.

A barrage of gunfire suddenly erupted from the target. Gunfire poured toward Ward and the *Sailfish*.

"Dive!" Ward shouted, suprised. The crew took the submarine back down below the water. There, Ward ordered his crew to reload the torpedo tubes.

The *Sailfish* and other American submarines not only attacked Japanese merchant and war ships, but also rescued many Allies from Pacific seas. Flyers who had been shot down and survivors of sinking ships were picked up by submarines in the area. This dramatic picture shows part of a rescue operation carried out by the submarines U.S.S. *Growler*, *Sealion*, *Barb*, *Queenfish*, and *Pampanito*. These submarines rescued 159 British and Australian prisoners of war and sank at least ten enemy ships. The rescue took place during enemy attacks and a raging typhoon.

Astor (above) is a torpedo capable of destroying submarines and surface vessels from greater distances than any presently operational torpedo. Unfortunately, it had not yet been developed for use during World War II.

The hours dragged on. Ward carefully brought the *Sailfish* back to the surface, hoping he wasn't coming up into another barrage of gunfire.

Finally, at eight o'clock in the morning, Ward saw his target for the first time. It was a Japanese aircraft carrier. The mighty ship sat unmoving in the water. Hordes of people swarmed on the aft deck. From the *Sailfish* Ward watched the people. They looked small, like ants running everywhere at once. They were all over the back of the ship.

"Fire!" Ward suddenly commanded.

Three more torpedoes shot out of the tubes. There was a swishing sound as the torpedoes zipped across the water just beneath the surface. Then they hit.

The ship was blown away. There was a horrible breaking sound. Great beams of timber crunched and cracked and came apart.

"Did you see what happened?" Ward yelled. As he stared out across the water he could see nothing because of the high waves. The waves pitched upward and heaved and fell again.

This torpedoed Japanese destroyer was photographed from the periscope of the *Nautilus*.

Another sinking ship seen through the periscope of an American submarine.

"Nothing!" shouted his officer. "I can't see anything!"

"Dive!" Ward suddenly commanded.

As he had been staring through the periscope, Ward suddenly saw a huge Japanese ship turn toward him. The ship had spotted the periscope and now was moving toward the sub. The ship charged straight at the submarine.

"I said dive!" shouted Ward. "Take her down to 90 feet!"

The *Sailfish* plunged beneath the water.

When it reached 90 feet, the sub leveled off. Far above, the huge Japanese ship moved across the water without striking the submarine.

"Reload," Ward commanded. The crew members reloaded the torpedo tubes. "Now, let's go up again," said Ward.

When Ward guided the *Sailfish* once more to the surface, the huge Japanese ship that had charged at him was gone. So was the slow-moving target Ward had tracked and sunk. That target had been the *Chuyo*. It now lay at the bottom of the ocean.

Later Bob Ward and the crew of the *Sailfish* were credited with being the first United States submarine to sink a Japanese aircraft carrier.

As 1943 ended, the Japanese were being clobbered with the heavy, devastating punches of American submarines. It was almost as if the

The crowded torpedo room of an American submarine. During the *Sailfish's* battle with the Japanese ships and the sinking of the *Chuyo*, there was frantic activity in the *Sailfish* torpedo room.

Americans had needed 1942 as an on-the-job training period. Now, with 1943 coming to an end, the entire Japanese shipping mechanism was crippled and limping badly. The country was suffering from the losses.

As the new year—1944—came in, the Pacific was crawling with deadly groups of submarines. The American subs were everywhere. They attacked and brought down enemy ships repeatedly.

The year 1944 proved just as successful as 1943 had been. It was so successful, in fact, that 1944 was the last year of the United States submarine war.

It was also the year that Herman Kossler, commander of the United States submarine *Cavalla*, ran into the biggest target of his life.

Kossler raised his periscope on June 19, 1944, in the Philippine Sea. He half expected to see nothing but the soft light of the summer sun on the water.

Herman Kossler, commander of the United States submarine *Cavalla*

That wasn't what happened, however. What he saw amazed him. He looked again through the periscope. There was no mistaking it. There sat the Japanese heavy cruiser *Shokaku*.

The Japanese ship had been around a long time. It was a veteran of Pearl Harbor and had survived the Battle of the Coral Sea.

Now it cruised along calmly. Kossler watched it through his periscope.

"We've got ourselves a big one," Kossler told his crew. He ordered the *Cavalla* into firing position.

"When I give the command," said Kossler, "fire six torpedoes at that sunofagun!"

"Yes, sir!" one of the crew replied.

"Fire!" commanded Kossler.

The six torpedoes zipped out of the tubes straight toward the *Shokaku*.

"Dive!" yelled Kossler. He had no intention of waiting around up there to see if he had hit the ship or not. The submarine aimed its nose downward and began a rapid descent.

As the *Cavalla* made its hasty dive, Kossler heard at least three of his torpedoes hit. He knew they had hit the ship. There was no doubt in his mind.

Then came the depth charges. Eight of them came straight down toward the *Cavalla*. The submarine continued to dive deeper. Still the depth charges came.

Submarine crews kept score of the ships they sank by painting flags on the submarines. A Japanese rising sun flag with rays stood for the sinking of a Japanese warship. A flag with the centered red sun on a white background stood for the sinking of a Japanese merchant ship.

They exploded and crashed around the submarine. The noise inside the submarine was deafening and terrifying. Still the depth charges came. More and more explosions ripped beneath the water.

The submarine was tossed around like a cork. The men cringed in fear, waiting for one of the charges to hit the sub and rip away their airlines.

The crippled Japanese ship, outraged, dropped depth charge after depth charge in a desperate attempt to kill the thing that had wounded her.

For three hours, more than a hundred depth charges fell around the *Cavalla*. Kossler kept taking his submarine deeper and deeper beneath the water. Finally he dived down deep enough to evade all of the charges. His submarine was not damaged.

As Kossler and his men waited below the water in safety, the great Japanese ship *Shokaku* died on the surface of the water. Four of Kossler's torpedoes had slammed into her. The ship fell out of formation and lay on the water's surface, burning out of control. Water flooded into the hanger space, through an elevator. Shortly after three o'clock that afternoon the great ship turned over on her side and plunged beneath the water, never to surface again.

By the end of that summer of 1944 the Japanese had been defeated in their fight with American submarines. The Japanese had lost numerous merchant ships and war ships. They could not be replaced.

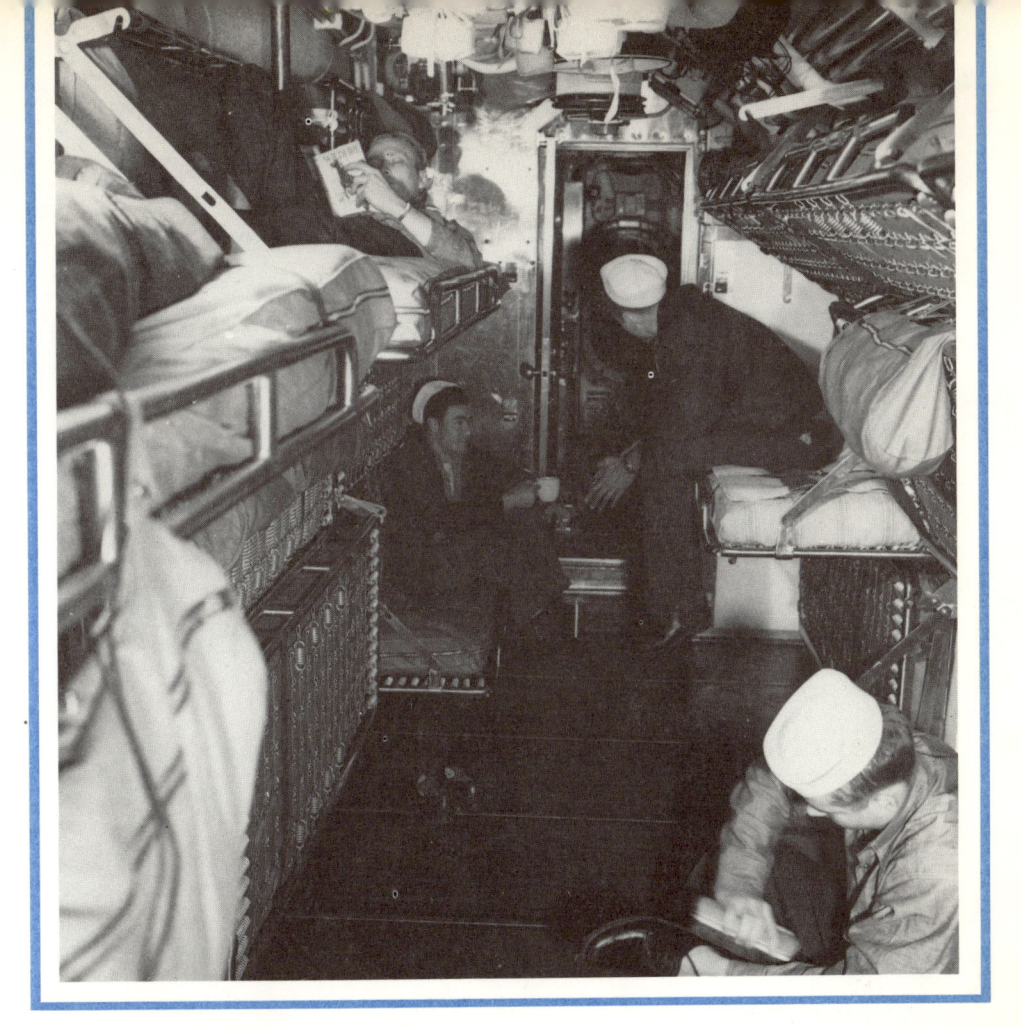

Crowded submarine bunkroom quarters

The entire course of the war in the Pacific had turned. The United States had learned to fight effectively beneath the waters of the Pacific Ocean.

Now it was all over. There was hardly anything left for the American submarine groups to attack. The few enemy ships that were left stayed well

43

within the safety of the borders of the Sea of Japan. Others were corralled in the Yellow Sea. They dared not venture out into the ocean. They contented themselves with running along close to the shorelines. At night they hid in harbors from the submarine groups that were on the prowl.

United States submarines had evolved into a fearsome fighting unit. They also distinguished themselves in rescue operations. One sub commander, Dick O'Kane, aboard his submarine the *Tang*, rescued more people than any other sub commander during the entire war. O'Kane made a daring run off Truk and came back with twenty-two airmen.

When the war was over and the United States Strategic Bombing Survey issued its report on the role of United States submarines during the war, the report stated:

"The war against shipping was perhaps the most decisive single factor in the collapse of the Japanese economy and logistic support of Japanese military and naval power. Submarines

Tang commanding officer Dick O'Kane with the twenty-two aircraft-carrier-based pilots who were rescued off Truk Lagoon.

accounted for the majority of vessel sinkings and the greater part of the reduction in tonnage."

In short, much of the success of the Pacific war was due to those rarely seen wolf packs that prowled beneath the sea.

45

The crew of the submarine *Archerfish* receives mail in port after returning from a war patrol.

About the Author

A native of Alabama, G.C. Skipper has traveled throughout the world, including Jamaica, Haiti, India, Argentina, the Bahamas, and Mexico. He has written several other children's books as well as an adult novel. Mr. Skipper has also published numerous articles in national magazines. He is now working on his second adult novel. Mr. Skipper and his family live in Norristown, Pennsylvania, a suburb of Philadelphia.

McDONOUGH MIDDLE SCHOOL LIBRARY

21456